NECRONOMIXOLOGY

BE WARNED!!!

By opening this book you are beginning a journey that will be filled with truly strange encounters. Only the _fearless_ should continue any further!

This bizarre journal contains a varied collection of creepy cocktails and chilling concoctions that have been created to allure both visually and in taste.

Even a novice mixologist will be able to craft these curious recipes and learn the secret art of conjuring unique mixed drinks and specialty shots.

If you follow this guide then you will be able to summon these same enticing intoxicants.

And hopefully, these tantalizing designs will also inspire you to bring your own evil creations to life.

A fundamental fact that should be stated
before continuing any further is this:
Everyone has their own preferences!

None of these recipes are set in stone
(they are just inked in human blood)
so they can always be altered to fit
the taste of whoever is consuming them.
Do not resist the urge to experiment with
different components, ratios and techniques
to discover what truly works best for you.

If you don't like a particular ingredient then
simply find a substitute for it. Just be aware that
some changes may drastically alter the end result.

For example: Changing cinnamon schnapps to
cinnamon whiskey within a dairy-based drink
will result in the whiskey curdling the cream.
So even a seemingly minor alteration can have a
very significant and sometimes undesired outcome.

But, trial and error is just part of creating.
Do not shy away from trying out odd combinations.
Endlessly explore the mad realms of possibility!

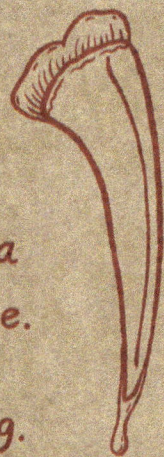

The Mixologist's Arsenal

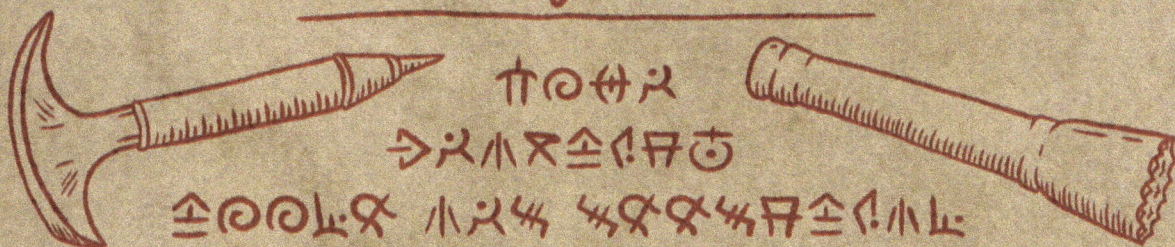

⇑⋔○⊕⋩
⋗⋏⋏⋌⋔⊂⋔⊙
⊆○○◡⋩ ⋏⋌⋎ ⋎⋩⋩⋎⋔⊆⋌⋏⌐

Another crucial element in creating exceptional mixtures is the equipment you use. You do not need the most expensive implements, but without the proper essentials, the magic you produce will only be so strong. These basics are required:

Blender
An electric appliance used
for grinding up ingredients.

Cobbler Shaker
A metal container used
for shaking up ingredients
(includes a built-in strainer).

Cocktail Picks
A small skewer used
for holding garnishes.

Jigger
A double-sided measuring
cup that holds 1 oz. and ½ oz.

Muddler
A pestle used for mashing
and stirring ingredients.

Acquiring additional tools (such as a cocktail spoon, mesh strainer, specific glassware, etc.) will make certain tasks easier and your creations will be even more impressive!

Ice Cubes

It may seem like an insignificant part of crafting, but the ice that you use will have a huge impact on the final taste and texture of your potions. Using quality ice, made from filtered water, is an important step in elevating all of your mixtures.

Standard ice cubes are the frozen forms that are primarily used, but there are other variations that will assist you in executing different icy results:

Cracked Ice

Hold an ice cube in the palm of your hand and then use the back of a cocktail spoon to bluntly smack the ice several times, until it cracks and breaks apart. You mainly want large chunks and not small shards.

Crushed Ice

Place ice cubes in the center of a clean tea towel and fold over the edges of the towel so that all of the ice is completely covered. Then use a wooden mallet to smash up the ice, until it is broken into small chunks.

Alternatively, you can create larger amounts of crushed ice by using a blender. Place a few cups of ice into the blender and use short bursts with the pulse button to break it all up. Strain out any excess water and serve (extra crushed ice can be stored in a freezer bag).

Dry Ice

This specialty ice will produce a cool smoke effect, but it can also be very dangerous. Always use proper safety precautions when handling this product. And, never directly touch or ingest any of the dry ice chunks!

Frosted Glass

Fill a glass with ice cubes and then pour in cold water. Then place the glass in the freezer for 6 minutes. Once it is frosted, pour out the ice and water and immediately prepare your mixed drink.

Ice Sphere

Use a silicone ice mold to create these large balls of ice. This form will also melt slower than ice cubes.

Basic Terminology

As you continue on, you will notice the repeated use of certain words that you should become familiar with. These key terms are used often but without additional instructions, so knowing their definitions will aid in your crafting speed and prowess.

Dash
About 10 drops of a liquid
(typically used for bitters).

Float
Delicately pouring a liquid on top
of another so that they do not mix
(Floating Technique - on next page).

Garnish
A decorative flourish that adds some
style to the drink. This embellishment
is usually edible and the final touch.

Muddle
To use a pestle to mash up ingredients
(typically fruit) at the bottom of a glass.

Pinch
An approximate amount of an ingredient
(typically a powder) that can be held
between your thumb and forefinger.

Rim
To coat the outer lip of a glass with a substance,
usually so that a garnish can be adhered to it.

Splash
Too much to be considered a dash and not
enough to be a real fraction of an ounce
(this quantity is more of a taste choice).

Top
Unlike a float, this pour is intended to mix
with the overall drink (usually for carbonated
liquids that should be gently mixed in).

Additionally, (as the name suggests) it can
also mean to fill the liquid to the top. If there
isn't a stated amount, then add to the drink
until it is nearly to the rim of the glass.

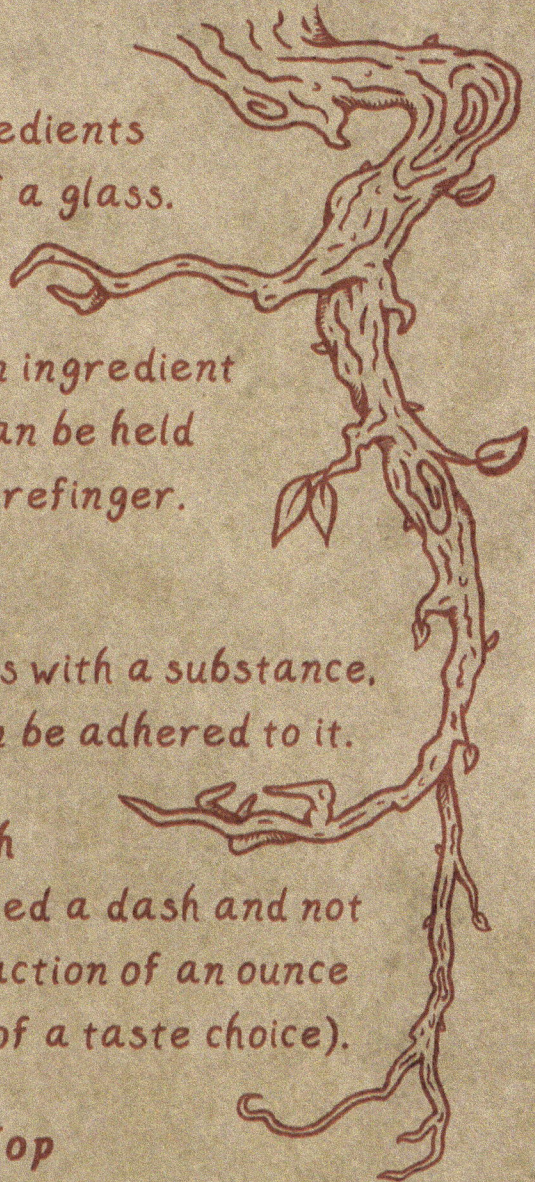

Floating Technique

Various tools can be used to achieve this effect,
but the method is pretty much the same for all of them.
Using a cocktail spoon or small butter knife is ideal.

You want to blunt the poured liquid's impact so that
it does not mix with the rest of the drink. Hold the
spoon at an angle so that it slants down towards the
drink's surface. Then slowly pour the liquid so it comes
in contact with the spoon before gently flowing off.

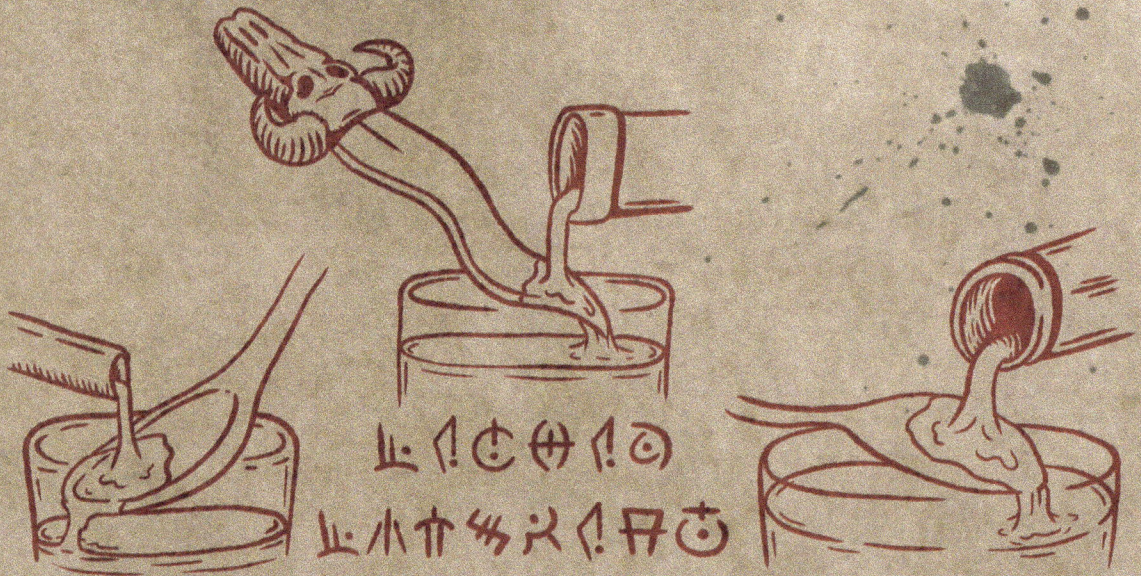

It takes some practice, but it also depends on the
weight and buoyancy of the liquids being used.

Typically, the higher the alcohol content, the
lighter the liquid will be. Due to this, it is impossible
to layer certain substances on top of others.

BEYOND THIS POINT
THERE IS NO TURNING BACK!

YOU WILL NEVER BE THE SAME!

ACID BLOB

This amorphous form appears to be both
solid and liquid. It dissolves itself so that
it can absorb its victim from the inside.

2 oz. Vodka
2 oz. Orange Juice
½ oz. Lime Juice
6 oz. Ginger Beer
Ice Cubes
Pink Cotton Candy

Steps:

1. Pour all liquid ingredients
   and ice into a glass mug.

2. Gently stir, if needed.

3. Garnish with a small fist size of cotton candy.
   (It will quickly dissolve into the drink and make it fizz.)

ALBINO ALLIGATOR

Watch out for this sleek, pale brute!
When it emerges, it will inflict a swift snap.

2 oz. White Rum
⅓ oz. Melon Liqueur
7 Cucumber Slices
7 Mint Leaves
3 oz. Club Soda
Splash of Lime Juice
Ice Cubes

Steps:

1. Put 6 cucumber slices, mint and lime juice into a shaker.

2. Muddle real well.

3. Add rum, melon liqueur and ice into the shaker.

4. Shake well and then strain into a highball glass with fresh ice.

5. Top with club soda and garnish with the final cucumber slice.

BLACK LAGOON

A unique creature lurks within these dark waters.
Bulging eyes emerge from the surface to stare back at you.

1 ½ oz. Blue Curaçao
2 oz. Vodka
6 oz. Lemonade
3 oz. Pineapple Juice
Activated Charcoal Tablet
Ice Cubes
Lime Wedge
2 Maraschino Cherries

Steps:

1. Pour all liquid ingredients into a shaker with ice.

2. Open the charcoal tablet and drop the powder in.

3. Shake well and strain into a hurricane glass
   with fresh crushed ice.

4. Garnish with the lime wedge and cherries.

BLOOD MOON RISING

It has been long believed that this crimson phenomenon contains powerful properties. Rituals have been conducted in its red shimmer.

2 oz. Moonshine
4 oz. Blood Orange Juice
½ oz. Raspberry Liqueur
1 oz. Cranberry Juice
Club Soda
Ice Cubes
Blood Orange Wheel

Steps:

1. Pour all liquid ingredients (except for club soda) and ice into a glass mason jar.

2. Cover the jar and shake well.

3. Uncover and top with club soda.

4. Garnish with the blood orange wheel.

BONEYARD BONFIRE

These burning flames can be felt deep within your soul.
Dance with rattling remains as the embers glow.

½ cup Heavy Cream
1½ tbs. Pumpkin Puree
½ tsp. Vanilla Extract
1 tsp. Pumpkin Pie Spice
1½ tsp. Powdered Sugar

½ oz. 151-Proof Rum
1 oz. Dark Rum
5 oz. Hot Brewed Coffee
   (or Hot Chocolate)
Lemon Juice
Sugar
Cinnamon

Steps:

1. Put the heavy cream, pumpkin puree, vanilla extract, pumpkin spice and sugar in a chilled bowl.

2. Whip together for 3 minutes - then chill until needed.

3. Rim a coupe glass with lemon juice (about an inch wide).

4. Cover the lemon juice in sugar until well coated.

5. Pour 151-proof rum into the coupe glass.

6. Carefully light the rum on fire and shower the flame with cinnamon until the rimmed sugar is caramelized.

7. Safely pour the hot coffee in to extinguish the flame.

8. Pour in the dark rum and stir together, if needed.

9. Spoon the whipped cream on top until evenly coated.

10. Garnish with more cinnamon sprinkled on top.

BRAIN MATTER

It might look like a mutilated brain floating in a jar, but it has the ability to telepathically control peoples' minds.

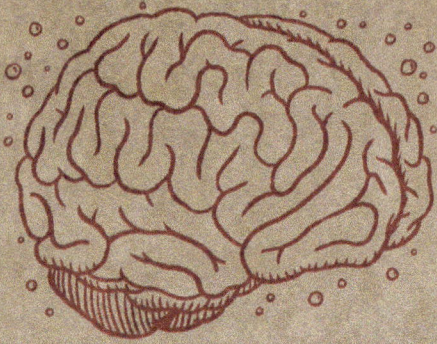

2 oz. White Rum
½ cup Blackberries,
     Raspberries
     & Strawberries
½ tsp. Honey
2 oz. Club Soda
Ice Cubes
Splash of Grenadine (optional)

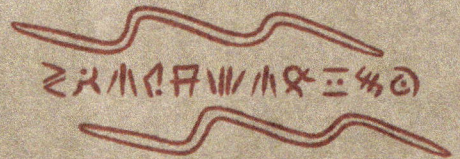

Steps:

1. Put all of the berries and honey in a rocks glass.

2. Muddle until the berries are thoroughly broken up.

3. Add rum and grenadine - muddle further, if necessary.

4. Add crushed ice and top with club soda.

5. Gently stir.

CULTURED CANNIBAL

This sophisticate has a disarming demeanor,
while also possessing a voracious taste for flesh.

2½ oz. Brandy
¾ oz. Dry Vermouth
½ oz. Amaretto
4 oz. Apple Cider
Dash of Angostura Bitters
Ice Cubes
Cooked Bacon Strip
(Applewood Smoked)

Steps:

1. Pour all liquid ingredients and ice into a shaker.

2. Shake well and then strain into a brandy glass.

3. Garnish with the bacon strip on a cocktail pick.

CORDIAL CANNIBAL

(Warm Version)

The same ingredients,
except for the ice.

Steps:

1. Heat up the cider in a sauce pan (until hot but not boiling).

2. Pour all of the other liquid ingredients into a mug.

3. Slowly pour the hot cider into the mug - stir, if needed.

4. Garnish with the bacon strip.

CYCLOPS' EYE

A sour eye attached to a full-bodied titan.
Harness its power and you'll be unstoppable,
but this giant is notoriously temperamental.

2 oz. Bourbon Whiskey
1 oz. Sweet Vermouth
1 oz. Lemon Juice
Dash of Angostura Bitters
2 oz. Dark Red Wine
    (Malbec or Merlot)
Ice Cubes
Lemon Wheel
Maraschino Cherry

Steps:

1. Pour all liquid ingredients (except for red wine) and ice into a shaker.

2. Shake well and then strain into a rocks glass with fresh ice.

3. Float the red wine or just pour it gently into the drink.

4. Garnish with a cocktail pick that has pierced the lemon wheel with the cherry in the center.

DARK DAZE

This mysterious cloud will entrance you with its stares.
Before you know it, your own eyes will be spinning.

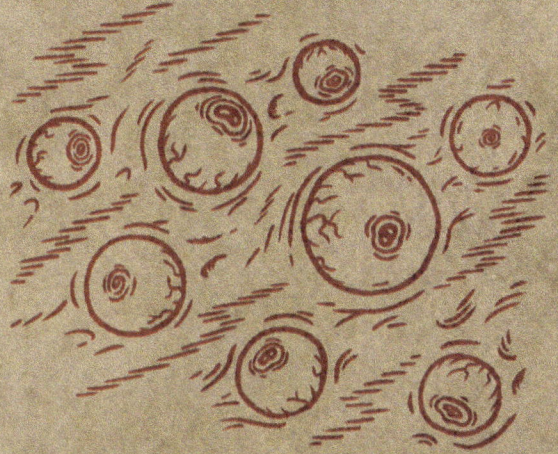

2 oz. Dark Rum
2 oz. Vodka
2 tsp. Black (or Brown)
    Sugar Syrup
5 oz. Black Iced Tea
1 oz. Milk
1/4 cup Tapioca Pearls
    (Black Sugar)
Ice Cubes

Steps:

1. Put tapioca pearls and ice into a highball glass.

2. Pour all liquid ingredients and ice into a shaker.

3. Shake well and strain into the highball glass.

DEMONIC TONIC

Those who ingest this fiery liquid possess
the soul of a demon. Only the most diabolical
will be able to withstand its scorching blaze.

1½ oz. Gin
½ oz. Absinthe
½ oz. Lemon Juice
4 oz. Tonic Water
Jalapeño Pepper
Cucumber
Ice Cubes
Mint Sprigs

Steps:

1. Slice up the cucumber (½ cup) - place a few slices to the side for later and put the rest in a shaker.

2. Slice the jalapeño in half long ways and then slice those halves in half short ways.

3. Deseed the jalapeño pieces - place the pointed halves to the side for later and put the rest in the shaker.

4. Muddle the cucumber slices and jalapeño halves in the shaker.

5. Add gin, absinthe, lemon juice and ice into the shaker.

6. Shake well and then strain into a highball glass with fresh ice.

7. Top with tonic - garnish with the mint sprigs, extra cucumber slices and pointed jalapeño halves.

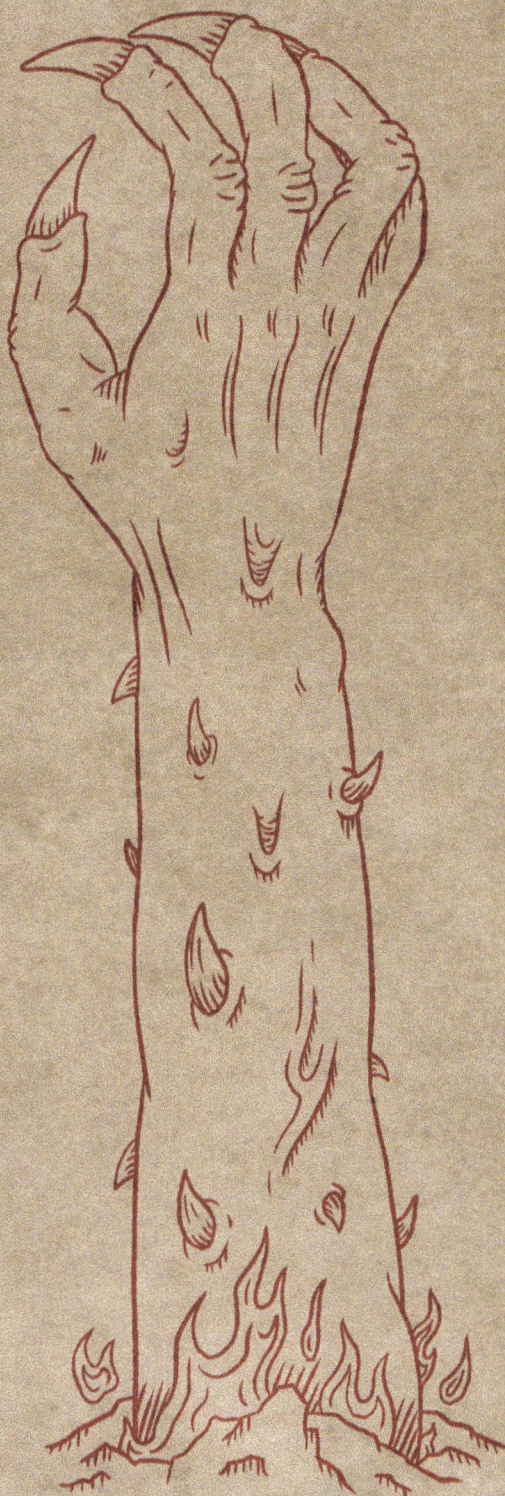

DUSK DOWNER

As the sun sinks down, the beasts hiding in the shadows emerge.
Absorbing this gloam will ward off those hungry night prowlers.

½ oz. Tequila
½ oz. Grand Marnier
½ oz. Ginger Ale
2 dashes of Lime Juice
2 dashes of Butterfly
   Pea Blossom Extract
Salt (optional)

Steps:

1. (Optional) Put the salt in a shallow dish.

2. (Optional) Rim a shot glass with extra lime juice.

3. (Optional) Dip the rim into the salt until evenly covered.

4. Pour Grand Marnier and lime juice into the shot glass.

5. Gently pour in the ginger ale and then the tequila.

6. Drop in the butterfly pea blossom extract, which
   will sink to the bottom and change the final coloring.

EVIL TWIN & GOOD TWIN

These two may look alike but they are polar opposites.
One is mild and sweet, while the other is shockingly sour.

Evil Twin

¾ oz. Limoncello
½ oz. Sour Apple Schnapps
¼ oz. Cinnamon Whiskey

Good Twin

½ oz. Creme de Banana
½ oz. Elderflower Liqueur
⅓ oz. Lemonade
⅙ oz. Midori

Steps:

1. Pour the "Evil Twin" ingredients into one shot glass and the "Good Twin" ingredients into another shot glass, then mix them around so that you don't know which shot is which.

2. Have a blind showdown with a friend and try to disguise your reactions - then have others try to identify which of you two is the "Evil Twin".

FOOLISH MORTAL

This portal is used to glimpse regions beyond our corporeal world, but do not linger or you might become trapped within.

2 oz. Vanilla Vodka
1 oz. Raspberry Liqueur
1 oz. Cranberry Juice
6 oz. Grape Soda
Pinch of Edible Glitter
½ cup Ice Cubes

Steps:

1. Thoroughly crush up the ice.

2. Put the crushed ice into a brandy glass.

3. Pour in all of the other ingredients.

4. Gently stir.

5. (Optional) Place a glowing ice cube in the center for extra effect.

FRANKEN-STEIN

A bizarre body constructed from an assortment
of parts. It may appear strange in look, but
it has a surprisingly gentle disposition.

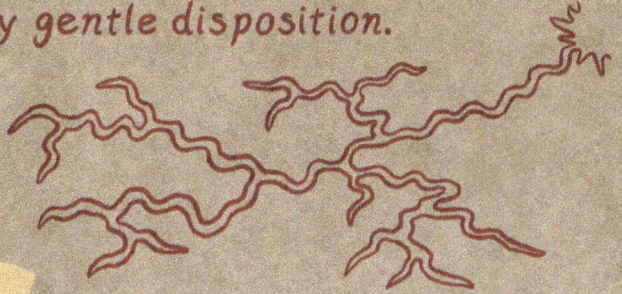

1 ½ oz. Midori
½ oz. Sour Apple Schnapps
1 oz. Vodka
½ oz. Triple Sec
2 oz. Lemonade
7 oz. Pale Lager

Steps:

1. Pour all liquid ingredients (except for
   the pale lager) into a frosted beer mug.

2. Stir well.

3. Gently pour pale lager into the glass.

FUNGAL FREAK

Don't be mislead by the fungus growing on this being,
it still has a very sharp bite. Take it slow around this one.

8 oz. Rye Whiskey

2 oz. Dried Shiitake
Mushrooms

3 drops of Angostura Bitters

2 drops of Amber Maple Syrup

Shiitake Mushroom (Raw or Dried)

Steps:

1. Put the whiskey and mushrooms into an airtight container.

2. Close tight, place in a cool dry area and let it infuse for 3 days.

3. Strain the whiskey into a bottle and refrigerate contents
   (it will keep for about 6 months). For larger quantities,
   simply duplicate the ratios and let it infuse for 6 days.

1. Pour 1½ oz. of mushroom-
   infused whiskey into a
   shot glass.

2. Add bitters and maple
   syrup - stir together.

3. Garnish with the
   Shiitake mushroom.

GASHADOKURO

This eerie white figure is an imposing presence.
Consume this spirit before it consumes you!

2 oz. Nigori Sake
1 ½ oz. Dry Gin
⅓ oz. Extra Dry
   Vermouth
Splash of Lychee Syrup
Ice Cubes
2 Lychee

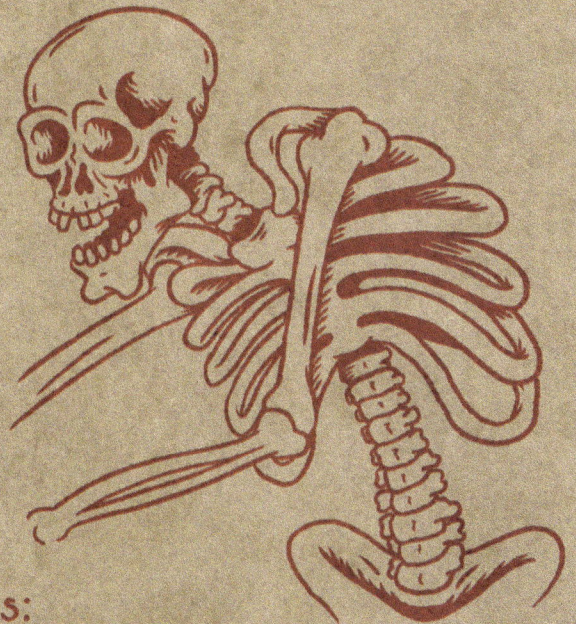

Steps:

1. Pour all liquid ingredients and ice into a shaker.

2. Shake well and then strain into a martini glass.

3. Garnish with the lychee pierced on a cocktail pick.

GIALLO

A vivid monument to terrifying thrillers, with a drop of blood at its center. Try to not obsess over this one too much.

1 oz. Galliano
1 oz. Limoncello
1 oz. Gin
½ tsp. Simple Syrup
Splash of Lemon Juice
Ice Cubes
Maraschino Cherry

⇑ ⅏ ⅃⅃ ⅃⅃ ◎ ⦀

Steps:

1. Pour all liquid ingredients and ice into a shaker.

2. Shake well and then strain into a martini glass.

3. Garnish with the cherry pierced on a cocktail pick.

GRIM REAPER

A tall, dark, chilling shape that is as old as time itself.
It's very patient and will collect from you when the time comes.

1 ½ oz. Southern Comfort
½ oz. Amaretto
½ oz. Triple Sec
6 oz. Cola
Ice Cubes

Steps:

1. Pour all ingredients into a highball glass.

2. Gently stir.

GRINDHOUSE

This stylized structure has a fairly gritty attitude.
Your personal taste may not find this one to be savory.

2 oz. Gin
½ oz. Dry Vermouth
½ cup Red Pepper
2 dashes of Hot Sauce
Splash of Lime Juice
Black Pepper
Ice Cubes
Cocktail Onion (optional)

Steps:

1. Cut up the red pepper into small chunks and then put into a shaker.

2. Muddle until peppers are thoroughly mashed up.

3. Pour all liquid ingredients and ice into the shaker.

4. Shake really well (at least a minute) and then strain into a martini glass.

5. Garnish with ground black pepper on top (optional) and the cocktail onion on a pick.

HEADLESS HORSEMAN

A vengeful being that has been decapitated and is searching for a replacement. Bring it close to your head at your own risk.

1 oz. Spiced Rum
8 oz. Pumpkin Ale
4 oz. Apple Cider
½ oz. 151-Proof Rum (optional)
Cinnamon (optional)

Steps:

1. Pour spiced rum and apple cider into a frosted pint glass.

2. Gently pour pumpkin ale into the glass (avoid any foam since this one is "headless").

3. (Optional) Gently float 151-proof rum on top.

4. (Optional) Carefully light the rum on fire and throw a pinch of cinnamon into the flame. Carefully exstinguish the flame before drinking.

HELL RISER

The high flames of this hellfire are oddly alluring and will draw its denizens back into it time and time again.

½ oz. Galliano
½ oz. Frangelico
½ oz. Irish Cream (Light)
Splash of Grenadine
Pinch of Nutmeg

Steps:

1. Pour Galliano and Frangelico into a shot glass.

2. Float the Irish cream on top.

3. Drop the grenadine through the Irish cream to create the flame effect.

4. Sprinkle the pumpkin pie spice on the surface of the Irish cream.

THE HONEYCOMB

An intriguing nectar that draws in the innocent before delivering a buzzing sting. You could be its next victim.

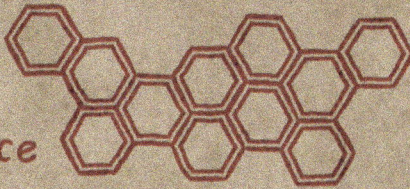  

2 oz. Vodka
1 oz. Lemon Juice
½ oz. Honey (or Hot Honey)
Egg Whites (1 Large Egg)
Pinch of Cinnamon
Ice Cubes

Steps:

1. Pour vodka, honey, lemon juice, and ice into a shaker.

2. Shake well and then strain into a coupe glass.

3. Put egg whites into a shaker.

4. Shake well ("dry shake" for 30 seconds).

5. Add ice into shaker and shake well again.

6. Strain and float onto the drink.

7. Garnish with cinnamon.

INHUMAN SOUL

The remnants of this person are very dark and bitter.
Swallowing this could warp and corrupt your own soul.

¼ oz. Gin
¼ oz. Campari
¼ oz. Blue Curaçao
¼ oz. Sweet Vermouth
½ oz. Club Soda

Steps:

1. Pour all ingredients (except club soda) into a shot glass.

2. Top with the club soda.

JEKYLL & RYE

Equal parts genial gentleman and macabre madman.
It would be wise to get on both of their good sides.

#1
1 oz. Rye Whiskey
3 oz. Cranberry Juice
½ oz. Blue Curaçao
Ice Cubes

#2
1 oz. Rye Whiskey
2 oz. Orange Juice
1 ½ oz. Ginger Ale
Ice Cubes

Steps:

1. Pour all #1 ingredients and ice into a shaker.

2. Shake well and strain into a highball glass.

3. Pour all #2 ingredients (except for ginger ale) and ice into a shaker.

4. Shake well and strain into a separate glass.

5. Add the ginger ale into the second mixture.

6. Float the second mixture on top of the first mixture.

JERSEY DEVIL

An extraordinary hybrid that loves to wreck havoc.
This abnormal creature continues to confuse and confound.

1 ½ oz. Moonshine
⅓ cup Frozen Blueberries
⅓ oz. Lime Juice
3 oz. Root Beer
2 oz. Club Soda
Root Beer Candy Stick

Steps:

1. Pour blueberries and lime juice into a rocks glass.

2. Muddle until berries are thoroughly broken up.

3. Pour in remaining liquid ingredients.

4. Garnish with the candy stick and gently stir.

KILLER CLOWN

It uses a colorful appearance to lure people in.
Be careful or it will get the best of you.

⅓ oz. Frangelico
½ oz. Vanilla Vodka
½ oz. Jägermeister
¼ oz. Limoncello
Honey
Sprinkles

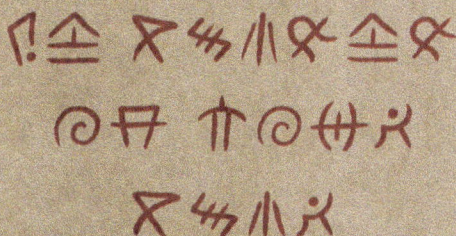

Steps:

1. Put the sprinkles in a shallow dish.

2. Rim a shot glass with the honey.

3. Dip the rim into the sprinkles until evenly covered.

4. Pour the liquid ingredients into the shot glass.

LAST CALL OF CTHULHU

Summoning this ancient leviathan can result in pure chaos!
Use extreme caution – or you may experience intense
hallucinations and slip into an abyss of absolute insanity!

1 ½ oz. Black Spiced Rum
⅓ oz. Absinthe
½ oz. Triple Sec
Splash of Lime Juice
7 oz. Ginger Beer
Ice Cubes
Lime

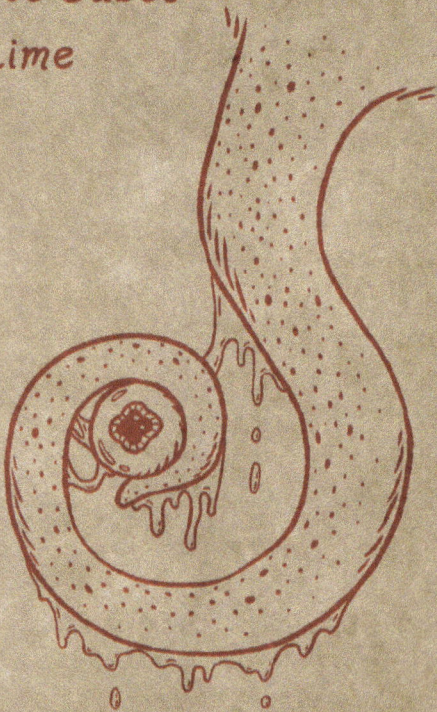

Steps:

1. Peel lime rind into strips and then cut a wedge.

2. Pour all liquid ingredients (except for ginger beer)
   and ice into a shaker.

3. Shake well and then strain into a highball glass with cracked ice.

4. Gently pour ginger beer into the mixture.

5. Garnish with the lime wedge and rind strips on the lip of the glass.

LAVA DROP

This fragment of molten fire can be melded into a bubbling flow that will imbue you with a blazing rush.

½ oz. Jägermeister
½ oz. Amaretto
⅓ oz. Cinnamon Whiskey
Splash of 151-Proof Rum
½ pint Pale Lager

Steps:

1. Pour pale lager into a pint glass.

2. Pour jägermeister, amaretto and whiskey into a shot glass.

3. Float 151-proof rum on top.

4. Carefully light the rum on fire and drop the entire shot glass into the pint glass and then chug the contents.

LYCANTHROPE

If you come in close contact with one of these unruly beasts, then a similar transformation may wash over you.

1 oz. Vodka
½ oz. Coffee Liqueur
½ oz. Creme de Cacao
1 ½ oz. Irish Cream
1 oz. Milk

2 tbsp. Creamy Peanut Butter
¼ cup Ice Cubes
1 tsp. Chocolate Syrup
Peanut Butter Cup
(White Chocolate)

Steps:

1. Place all ingredients (except for chocolate syrup and peanut butter cup) into a blender.

2. Before blending, drizzle the chocolate syrup inside of a coupe glass.

3. Blend well and then pour into the coupe glass.

4. Garnish with the peanut butter cup on the rim.

MEAN GREEN MONSTER

A carnivorous plant that likes to feed on human flesh.
If you take a nip from it then it might just nip you back.

ᛉ ⚡⚡ ⚡⚡ ©
ᛉ ᛉ ⚡⚡

2 oz. Tequila

3 Kiwi

½ oz. Lime Juice

1 oz. Triple Sec

½ tsp. Simple Syrup

Mint Sprigs

Jalapeño Pepper

Salt

¾ cup Ice Cubes

2 oz Coconut Milk
    (optional - less spicy version)

Steps:

1. Put the salt in a shallow dish.

2. Rim a margarita glass with lime juice.

3. Dip the rim into the salt until evenly covered.

4. Peel and slice all of the kiwi (put 2 wedges to the side).

5. Slice up ⅙ of the jalapeño.

6. Put the sliced kiwi, sliced jalapeño, lime juice, triple sec, simple syrup and 2 mint leaves in a blender.

7. Blend until smoothly pureed and then add in the tequila and ice cubes (and optional coconut milk).

8. Blend again until it's a slushy consistency and then pour into the margarita glass.

9. Garnish using the extra kiwi wedges and mint sprigs.

MOTHMAN

Two gleaming red eyes nestled within a mysterious silhouette.
This legend will sneak up on you by blending in with the night.

1 ½ oz. Black Raspberry
Liqueur
½ oz. Blue Curaçao
2 oz. Cranberry Juice
8 oz. Wheat Beer
Ice Cubes
2 Maraschino Cherries

Steps:

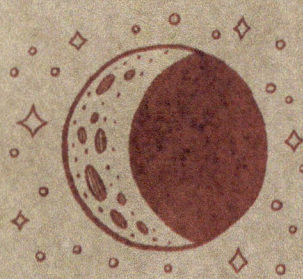

1. Pour all liquid ingredients (except for beer) and cracked ice into a highball glass.

2. Gently pour in beer, stir if necessary.

3. Garnish with the two cherries.

MURDER OF CROWS

A mass of black that moves as one to envelope its prey.
After it disperses, there's a drained husk and nothing more.

2 oz. Tequila
1 oz. Blue Curaçao
1 cup Frozen Black Cherries,
    Blackberries and
    Black Raspberries
1 ½ oz. Cranberry Juice
½ oz. Lime Juice
½ oz. Lemon Juice
1 Activated Charcoal Tablet
7 oz. Pale Lager (mini bottle)
¼ oz. Grenadine

Steps:

1. Pour all ingredients (except for the pale lager and grenadine) into a blender.

2. Blend until smooth.

3. Slowly pour through a mesh strainer (to remove seeds) into a margarita glass.

4. Pour the grenadine into the pale lager bottle.

5. Quickly and carefully dunk the mini bottle into the margarita drink so that it's nearly upside down.

NIGHTMARE FUEL

This ring of salt can trap shadowy night terrors.
Their energy can then be absorbed for your own use.

1½ oz. Tequila
½ oz. Coffee Liqueur
6 oz. Cola
Lime Juice
Salt
Ice Cubes

Steps:

1. Put the salt in a shallow dish.

2. Rim a rocks glass with lime juice.

3. Dip the rim into the salt until evenly covered.

4. Pour tequila, coffee liqueur, cola and ice into a rocks glass.

5. Gently stir, if needed.

ONE-EYED DREAM-DEMON

Don't be fooled by this charming fellow. If you're not mindful, he will use illusions to trick you into a binding contract.

1 ½ oz. Bourbon Whiskey
½ oz. Elderflower Liqueur
⅓ oz. Goldschläger
2 dashes of Orange Bitters
Orange Rind
Ice Cubes
Large Ice Sphere

Steps:

1. Pour all liquid ingredients and ice into a mixing glass.

2. Stir well to dilute and then strain into a rocks glass with an ice sphere.

3. Carefully hold a flame above the glass and lightly toast the orange rind before squeezing it so that the spraying oils ignite over the drink.

4. Rub the rind around the rim of the glass.

POSSESSION POTION

Consuming this powerful elixir can cause a sudden transference of consciousness into a different body.

⅓ oz. Coconut Rum
⅓ oz. Blue Curaçao
⅓ oz. Creme de Banana
½ oz. Pineapple Juice
Splash of 151-Proof Rum
Cinnamon

Steps:

1. Pour all ingredients (except for 151-proof rum and cinnamon) into a shot glass.

2. Float the 151-proof rum on top and then carefully light it on fire.

3. Sprinkle a pinch of cinnamon into the flame and then carefully exstinguish it.

PSYCHO CHILLER

It may have a fairly simple appearance, but a grim and complex secret resides within this cold-hearted soul.

1 ½ oz. Vodka
½ oz. Creme de Cacao
½ oz. Black Sesame Syrup
2 oz. Heavy Cream
½ oz. Frangelico
Black Sesame Seeds
Ice Cubes

Steps:

1. Pour vodka, creme de cacao and sesame syrup into a rocks glass with crushed ice.

2. Stir well and then put to the side.

3. Pour the heavy cream and Frangelico into a mixing glass.

4. Stir well and then gently pour over the drink.

5. Garnish by showering the drink with the sesame seeds.

QUARANTINI SLAMMER

A solution is held within this bubbly tincture
and it could be a remedy for what's ailing you.

²/₃ oz. Vodka
½ oz. Sour Apple Schnapps
⅓ oz. Cinnamon Schnapps
½ oz. Club Soda

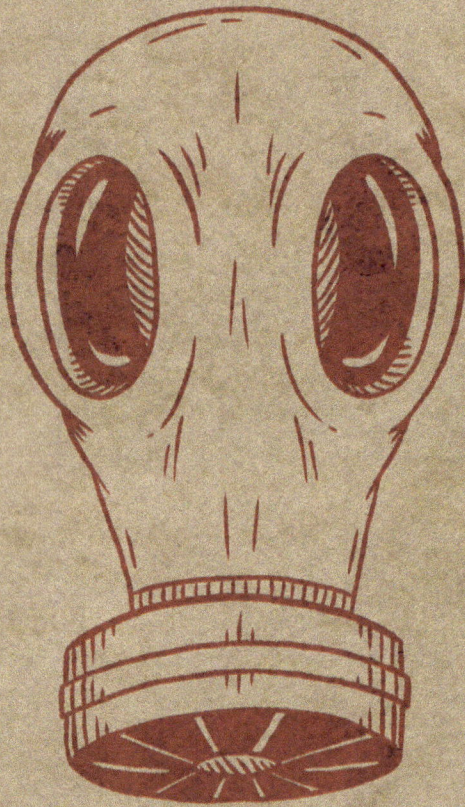

Steps:

1. Pour all ingredients
   (except for club soda)
   into a tall shot glass.

2. Top with the club soda.

RADIOACTIVE WASTE

This glowing substance has the strange ability to mutate whatever is exposed to it.

1 ½ oz. Bourbon Whiskey
1 ½ oz. Midori
½ oz. Lime Juice
½ oz. Lemon Juice
Club Soda
Egg Whites (2 Eggs)
Ice Cubes

Steps:

1. Pour all ingredients (except for club soda and eggs) into a shaker.

2. Shake well and strain into a highball glass.

3. Top with club soda.

4. Put egg whites into a shaker.

5. Shake well ("dry shake" for 30 seconds).

6. Add ice into shaker and shake well again.

7. Strain and float onto the drink.

REANIMATOR

This slender tube contains a bright mixture that can inject new vigor into a lifeless person.

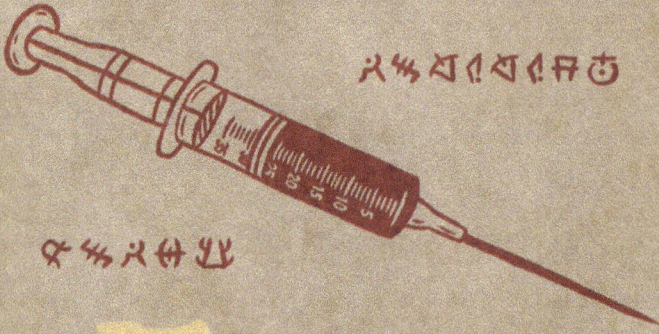

1 oz. Bourbon Whiskey
½ oz. Grand Marnier
2 oz. Passion Fruit Juice
¼ oz. Blue Curaçao
Sparkling Wine (Dry)
Ice Cubes
Small Lime Wedge

Steps:

1. Pour all liquid ingredients (except for sparkling wine) and ice into a shaker.

2. Shake well and then strain into a highball glass.

3. Top with the sparkling wine.

4. Garnish with the lime wedge.

REDRUM

This intense individual has a bold and aggressive attitude.
Dealing with them may be an acquired taste.

2 oz. Dark Rum
1 oz. Campari
1 oz. Sweet Red
    Vermouth
Ice Cubes

Steps:

1. Pour all ingredients into a mixing glass.

2. Stir well to dilute the ingredients.

3. Strain into a rocks glass with fresh ice.

SCREAM QUEEN

A very sweet figure who is chilled to the core.
This one will certainly produce a blood-curdling shriek.

2 oz. Coconut Rum
2 oz. Gold Rum
½ oz. Triple Sec
4 oz. Lemonade
2 oz. Coconut Cream
1 cup Frozen Strawberries
     and Pineapple Chunks
½ cup Ice Cubes
1 tsp. Grenadine
Pineapple wedge

Steps:

1. Pour all ingredients (except for grenadine and pineapple wedge) into a blender.

2. Before blending, drizzle the grenadine on the inside of a hurricane glass.

3. Blend well and then pour into the glass.

4. Garnish with the pineapple wedge on the rim.

THE SEVEN DEADLIES

Lust, Gluttony, Envy, Pride, Sloth, Greed and Wrath.
This allows you to commit every single sin all at once!

⅓ oz. Grenadine
⅓ oz. Creme de Cacao
⅓ oz. Creme de Menthe
⅓ oz. Blue Curaçao
⅓ oz. Irish Cream
⅓ oz. Goldschläger
⅓ oz. Jägermeister

Steps:

1. Pour the grenadine into a tall shot glass.

2. Float the creme de cacao on top of that.

3. Float the creme de menthe on top of that.

4. Float the blue curaçao on top of that.

5. Float the Irish cream on top of that.

6. Float the Goldschläger on top of that.

7. Float the Jägermeister on top of that.

SLASHER

A bloody massacre with a thoroughly sliced up body.
Anyone who sticks around for too long will be slayed.

"Final Girl" (serving for 1)

1 ½ oz. Brandy
5 oz. Red Wine (Pinot Noir)
3 oz. Apple Cider
1 oz. Orange Juice
Splash of Lemon Juice
Dash of Angostura Bitters
Ice Cubes
¼ Red Apple (Gala)
Pinch of Cinnamon

"Campers" (serving for 6)

1 cup Brandy
1 bottle of Red Wine
    (Pinot Noir)
2 cups Apple Cider
6 oz. Orange Juice
1 oz. Lemon Juice
4 dashes of Angostura
    Bitters
Ice Cubes
1 ½ Red Apple (Gala)
Pinches of Cinnamon

"Final Girl" Steps:

1. Slice up the apple into thin pieces and then dice up those slices into small chunks.

2. Put the apple chunks into a stemless wine glass.

3. Pour all of the liquid ingredients into the glass.

4. Add ice and stir well.

5. Refigerate for at least 2 hours so that the apples can marinate.

6. Garnish with the cinnamon.   ⊵⊾⋦⋦☉⟨⊞☡

"Campers" Steps:

1. Slice up the apples into thin pieces and then dice up those slices into small chunks.

2. Put the apple chunks into a glass pitcher.

3. Pour all of the liquid ingredients into the pitcher.

4. Add ice and stir well.

5. Refigerate for at least 5 hours so that the apples can marinate (overnight is even better and the mixture will keep for about 3 days).

6. Serve in stemless wine glasses and garnish each drink with the cinnamon.

SPIDER SAC

Devouring this submerged spore will cause a tingling sensation that will spread over your entire body.

¾ oz. Gin
½ oz. Elderflower Liqueur
¼ oz. Yellow Chartreuse
2 drops of Orange Bitters
1 Blackberry

Steps:

1. Pour all liquid ingredients into a shot glass.

2. Stir, if needed.

3. Gently drop in the blackberry.

TINY TERROR

This little minion is actually a big troublemaker.
It's hyper attitude will keep you up all night!

¼ oz. Absinthe
⅓ oz. Galliano
⅔ oz. Coffee Liqueur
½ oz. Irish Cream

Steps:

1. Rinse a shot glass with the absinthe and then discard the excess liquid.

2. Pour in the Galliano and coffee liqueur.

3. Float the Irish cream on top.

TRANSMUTATOR

A shapeshifter that can alter its appearance in an instant.
Don't blink or you might just miss the transformation.

½ pint Pale Lager
⅓ oz. Blue Curaçao
⅔ oz. Raspberry
　　　Liqueur
½ oz. Scotch
　　　Whiskey

Steps:

1. Pour the pale lager into a pint glass.

2. Pour all of the other ingredients into a shot glass.

3. Drop the entire shot glass into the pint glass and then chug the contents.

TWISTED GRIN

This warped expression seems to hover in midair and is sure to give you a similarly deranged smile.

#1
1 cup of Frozen Raspberries
1½ oz. Raspberry Liqueur
1 oz. Tequila
2 oz. Cranberry Juice

#2
1 cup of Frozen Peaches
1½ oz. Peach Schnapps
1 oz. Light Rum
2 oz. Orange Juice

Steps:

1. Pour all #1 ingredients into a blender.

2. Blend until smooth - then put to the side.

3. Pour all #2 ingredients into a blender.

4. Blend until smooth.

5. Alternate pouring the two mixtures into a margarita glass (pour #1 through a mesh strainer to remove seeds).

6. Use a straw to slightly stir up the mixture.

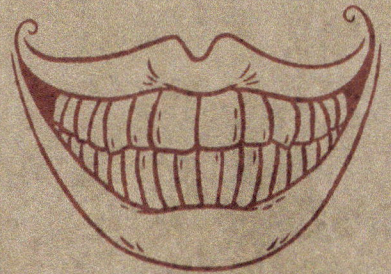

UGLY MUG

A strong curiosity surrounds this one, but a hideously puckered face is hidden behind the elegant façade.

⅔ oz. Limoncello
½ oz. Southern Comfort
⅓ oz. Peach Schnapps
Splash of Lime Juice
Sour Sugar

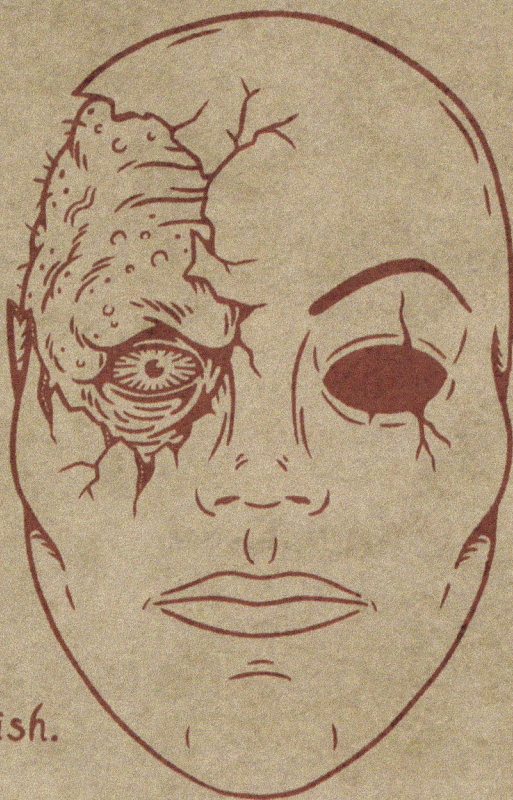

Steps:

1. Put the sour sugar in a shallow dish.

2. Rim a shot glass with extra lime juice.

3. Dip the rim into the sugar until evenly covered.

4. Pour the liquid ingredients into the shot glass.

UNDERSEA SHOCK

A beguiling glow emits from the depths of the drink.
Discover the secrets hidden beneath the surface.

1 ½ oz. Gin
6 oz. Pilsner
¼ oz. Blue Curaçao
½ oz. Lemon Juice
½ tbsp. Simple Syrup
Ice Cubes
Lemon Wedge
Mint Sprig

ꟷ⍓⦶⍓⦶⎔ ⇑⦶⋔ ⍑⏁⋔⦶⍓⏁

Steps:

1. Pour gin, lemon juice, simple syrups and ice into a shaker.

2. Shake well and then strain into a highball glass.

3. Gently pour in the pilsner.

4. Gently drop in the blue curaçao.

5. Garnish with the wedge and sprig.

VAMPIRE'S KISS

A favorite of those who lurk in the shadows.
The seductive taste is accompanied by a small bite.

⅓ oz. Amaretto
⅓ oz. Creme de Cacao
½ oz. Tequila (Añejo Red)
⅓ oz. Cranberry Juice

Steps:

1. Pour all ingredients into a shot glass.

2. Mix together, if necessary.

VIAL OF VENOM

A shot from this vicious viper's bite
will bring on some truly potent effects.

1 oz. Vodka
¾ oz. Pickle Brine (Dill)
Ice Cubes
Dash of Hot Sauce

Steps:

1. Pour all ingredients into a shaker.

2. Shake well and then strain into a tall shot glass.

WAILING BANSHEE

This misty apparition will send a piercing shiver down your spine with its petrifying presence.

1 ½ oz. Irish Whiskey
1 oz. Blue Curaçao
6 oz. Lemonade
3 oz. Club Soda
Splash of Grenadine
Ice Cubes
Dry Ice (optional)

Steps:

1. Pour all of the liquid ingredients (except for club soda and grenadine) and ice into a highball glass.

2. Stir well.

3. (Optional) Carefully add dry ice to the bottom of the drink for an added smoke effect. Do not directly touch or ingest the dry ice chunks!

4. Top with the club soda and then drop in the grenadine.

WENDIGO BLOOD

Ingesting this spirit's essence will cause you
to be cursed with the same insatiable craving.

2 oz. Canadian Whiskey
1 tsp. Maple Syrup
1 tsp. Worcestershire Sauce
6 oz. Vegetable Juice
Dash of Hot Sauce (optional)
Pinch of Salt
Ice Cubes
2 Rosemary Sprigs
2 Cocktail Onions

Steps:

1. Pour all of the liquid
   ingredients, salt and
   ice into a shaker.

2. Shake well and then
   strain into a highball
   glass with cracked ice.

3. Garnish with the
   rosemary sprigs
   and the cocktail
   onions on a pick.

WITCH'S BREW

You can conjure this bubbly potion by using witchcraft.
An enchanted spell will wash over all who consume it.

1½ oz. Marshmallow Creme
½ oz. Heavy Cream
½ oz. Irish Cream
½ oz. Vanilla Vodka
1 oz. Butterscotch Schnapps
8 oz. Amber Ale
   (or Brown Ale)
4 oz. Cream Soda

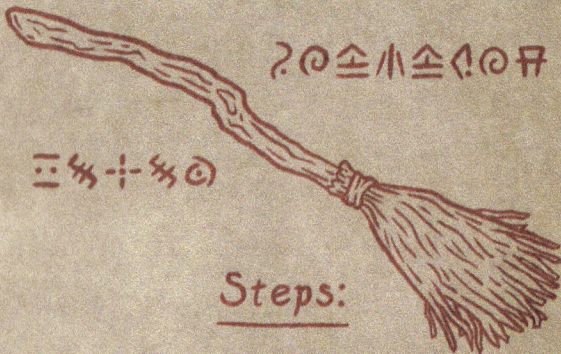

Steps:

1. Pour marshmallow creme, heavy cream, Irish cream and vodka into a small bowl.

2. Whisk together until smooth – put to the side for later.

3. Pour schnapps, ale and soda into a frosted beer mug.

4. Float the whisked cream on top.

XENO-EGGS

These alien spawn vessels are silently gestating as they wait for an unsuspecting host to approach.

1 oz. Midori
2 oz. Coconut Rum
8 oz. Watermelon Seltzer
3-4 Lychee

Steps:

1. Place the lychee (with the openings facing up) at the bottom of a frosted highball glass.

2. Pour in the Midori and rum - so that the lychee are submerged but not disturbed.

3. Gently top with the watermelon seltzer.

YETI HOWL

An icy chill will shoot through you when the fierce bellow of this snow beast hits you.

½ oz. Brandy
⅓ oz. Frangelico
⅓ oz. Creme de Banana
⅓ oz. Creme de Menthe

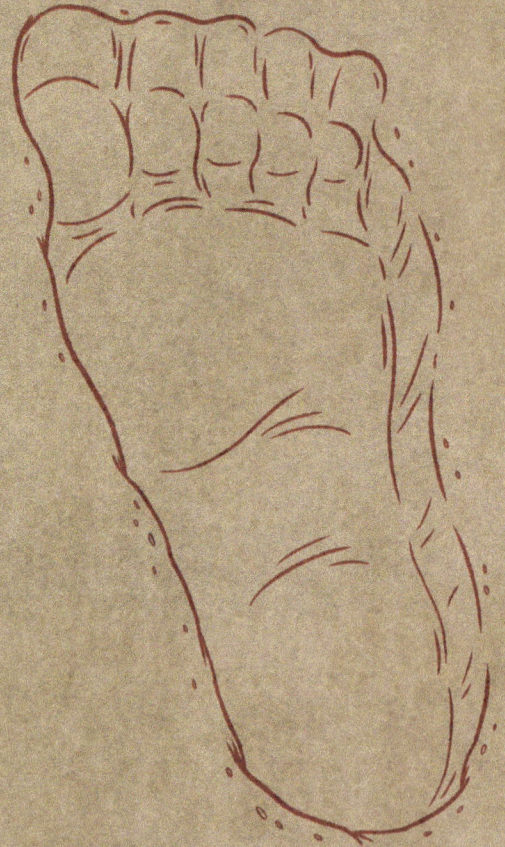

Steps:

1. Pour all ingredients into a shot glass.

2. Mix together, if necessary.

YULE GHOUL

This bringer of holiday fear will punish those who have misbehaved, so try to stay on its warm side.

6 oz. Red Wine (Zinfandel)
1 oz. Brandy
½ oz. Triple Sec
⅓ oz. Cinnamon Schnapps
1-2 Whole Cloves
2 tsp. Black Loose Leaf Tea
Orange Wedge
Cane Sugar
Cinnamon Stick

Steps:

1. Pour liquid ingredients, cloves and tea leaves into a sauce pan and heat up for 5 minutes (stir occasionally and do not let it boil).

2. Put the cane sugar in a shallow dish.

3. Rim a glass mug using the orange wedge.

4. Dip the rim into the sugar until evenly covered.

5. Slowly pour the hot liquid through a mesh strainer (to remove cloves and tea leaves) into the mug.

6. Garnish with the orange wedge and cinnamon stick.

ZOMBIE KING

The ultimate ruler of the undead! This golden grave riser has total control over all other living corpses.

1 ½ oz. Light Rum
1 ½ oz. Dark Rum
1 oz. Gold Rum
½ oz. Triple Sec
2 oz. Pineapple Juice
2 oz. Guava Juice
2 oz. Passion Fruit Juice
2 dashes of Angostura Bitters
¼ oz. Lemon Juice
¼ oz. Lime Juice
Splash of Grenadine
Club Soda
Ice Cubes
Pinch of Cinnamon
2 Maraschino Cherries
Mint Sprig
Lime Wedge

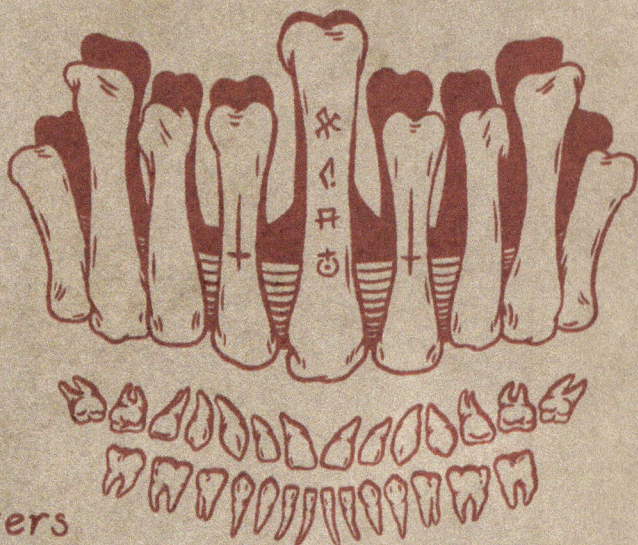

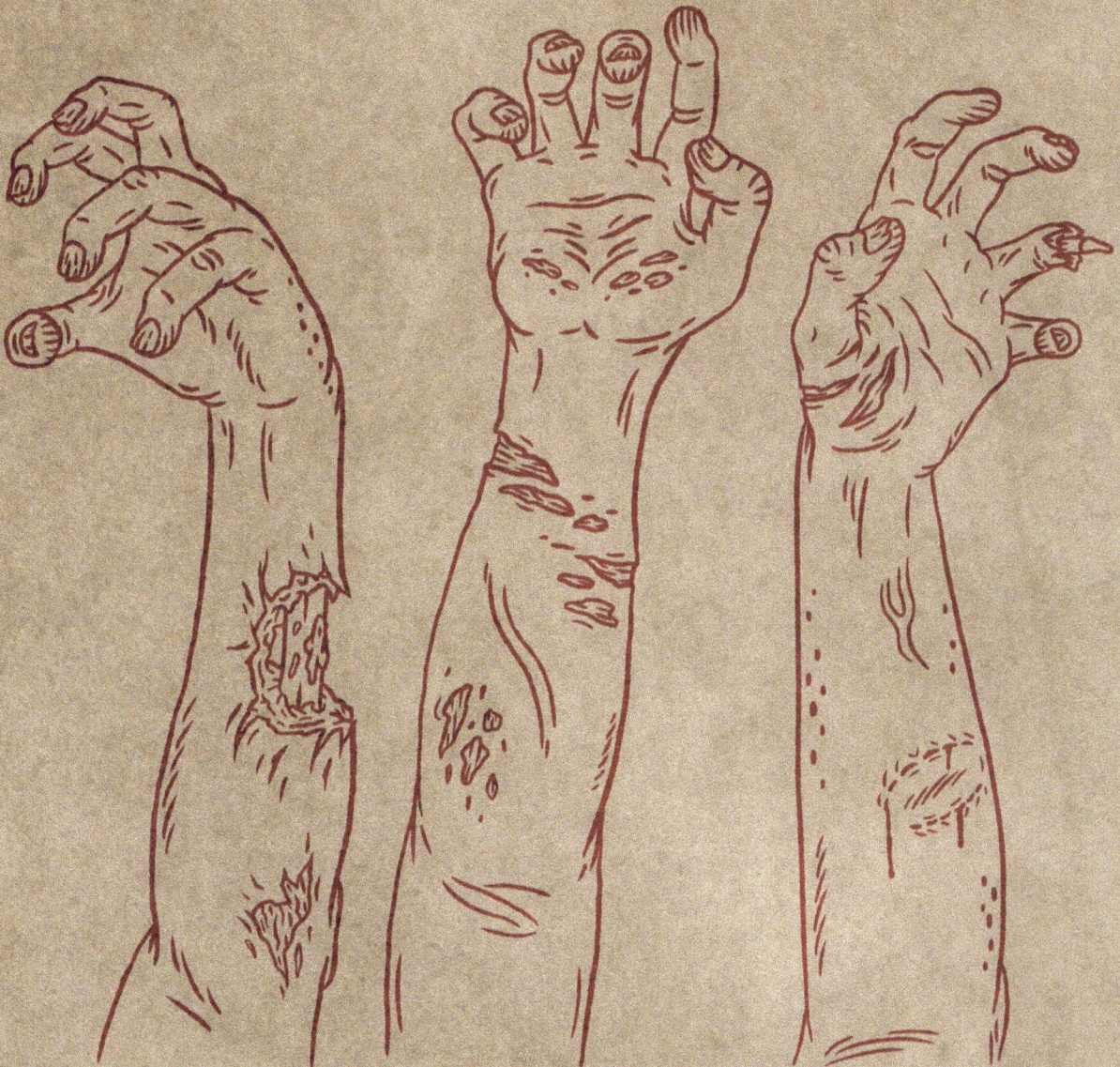

Steps:

1. Pour all liquid ingredients (except for the club soda) and ice into a shaker.

2. Shake well and then strain into a tiki mug with cracked ice.

3. Top with the club soda and sprinkle the cinnamon on top.

4. Garnish with the cherries, mint sprig and lime wedge.

THIS WAS MERELY A GLIMPSE OF WHAT
LIES WITHIN THIS INFINITE DIMENSION...

EVEN MORE CHAOS CAN BE CREATED
WITH THE IMMENSE POWER OF SPIRITS!

If you are somehow reading this, then you have miraculously made it through this entire book without going utterly mad!

And if that is true, then your bizarre journey does not have to end here. You should continue to experiment and master methods that are beyond these pages.

There is a vast realm of mixology that can still be explored and expanded upon. Try out recipes and techniques of your very own. You might even create something that has never been experienced before.

You have your own distinct taste and skills, so utilize those abilities to make something extraordinary!

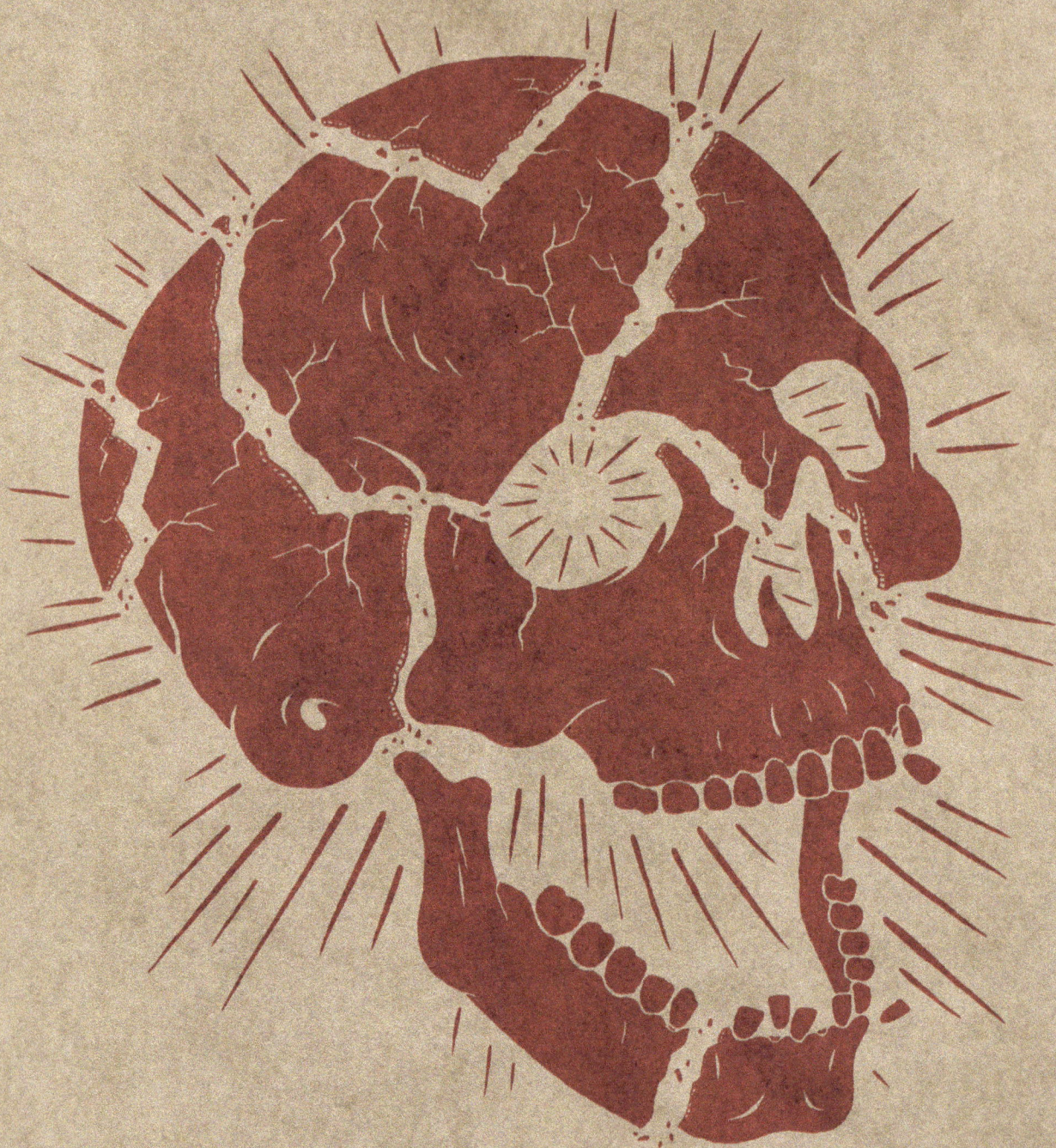

ISBN: 978-0-578-29109-3

NECRONOMIXOLOGY
Created by: Anthony Maddaloni